No Money No Ministry

Building Income to Fund your God Given Dreams

Pete Vossler

Library of Congress Control Number: 2024949062

Contents

Introduction

Are you tired of bake sales, fundraiser auctions, raffles, car washes, and parking lot sales...? So was I.

Many years ago, I went to an afternoon speaker symposium to hear one of my heroes of the faith, Jack Hayford, speak. For those who do not recognize the name, Jack Hayford was a Foursquare senior pastor of a great church in Van Nuys, California, during the Jesus revolution. Before it was popular and thought doable, his church was a multi-site, mega-church. As I sat there, listening and hanging on to every word, I realized that this quote changed my focus on creating income to fund my God-given dreams and changed me as a person of faith. Here it is, "during the great awakening in the Southern California. The church was so shaken that 98% of their members gave a tithe for God's glory."

Time stopped, and I do not remember anything spoken after that word. I said in my spirit, "If God is no respecter of persons (Romans 2:11), then why not me?" I had developed the thought that 100% tithe and offering of every constituent under my care was not "pie in the sky" but possible. I asked the Lord to teach me how, so the journey began.

Most people with a divine call from God have great dreams and visions of what, when, and how to fulfill their calling. It

1

doesn't matter if you are a minister, an associate minister, a missionary support staff member, or have a leadership position in a nonprofit; you have asked, "How am I going to fund this God-given dream?" This devotional is about creating the funding to complete the task buried in one's spirit.

I am retired after 40 years of senior leadership at the time of this writing. We had seen our mission giving grow 10X, and our tithe multiplied exponentially. With an upward trajectory, we realized 85% participation in giving in our larger congregation in a low—to lower-middle-income community.

The synopsis of this holy and foundational belief is that one hundred percent tithe and offering participation is doable. Any leader with the will to create funding for their dream can do it, and God would not place the dream in you if you didn't have the funds. It takes tenacity and a will to achieve it, but you can do it.

This devotional is for 30 days. This allows a leader to consume it in bite-size pieces, go through it daily for 30 days, and repeat as often as needed to implement the steps. So, let us begin.

Day 1

No Money, No Ministry

- Jeremiah 29:11

"For I know the plans I have for you, says the Lord, plans to prosper and not to harm you, plans to give you hope and a bright future."

The people of God were in captivity, and the Lord encouraged them through Jeremiah, the prophet, that where they are now is not his plan for their future.

Every leader must ask themselves the question before asking others to help them fund their vision. Why do I want to achieve my life dreams and visions? That question sounds pretty simple, right?

Do you want to achieve because you want to brag, show off, let somebody know you are somebody, stroke an insecurity, and show those above you that you are in their league? Your why should be that if nobody ever sees or knows how well you are doing, it is not by my power but by his spirit that you will happily give your all and be satisfied with your life dreams.

3

Challenge yourself now. Look inside your spirit and allow a real verbal moment between you and your heavenly father. When you are ready and have communicated with the Lord, proceed to more incredible things, and let's create a great Sunday and everyday giving machine.

ACTION STEP:

Write your why down, see it, and begin to believe it.

Day 2

What is my belief?

- 2 Cor. 9:11

"You will be made rich in every way so you can be generous on every occasion, and through us, your generosity will bring glory to God."

Those of us responsible for publicly speaking words that we believe are from the Holy Spirit have a moral authority to say words that we feel and think from the bottom of our hearts and minds. I am a proponent of the idea that people can tell in their subconscious minds if the speaker does not believe the words they are trying to teach.

Asking people to form or join your team with their finances deserves your utmost belief in the word of God; believe that it is God's will and that generosity is God's way of funding his kingdom's progress. Do you practice what you are about to teach? If not, it's game over; let's call it a day and move on to do something you believe in wholeheartedly, but you still have a problem: no money, no ministry.

When we speak about money, there can be no doubt of God's way, and the Old Testament and New Testament are two of your top priorities. No doubt, I want to leave you with a thought that has driven me to believe that 100% giving of a tithe in our mission is possible. A person cannot call themselves a fully devoted follower of Christ if they are not motivated by generosity; this is the very essence of our heavenly Father. He is a generous God who created us with generosity.

ACTION STEP:

Read Second Corinthians 9:6-11 and challenge yourself to start a 100% belief in his truth.

Day 3

Know your numbers

- Psalms 90:12

"Teach us to number our days aright so we may gain a heart of wisdom."

Many nonprofits trying to develop income streams to fund their vision fail because they lack clarity on the starting point and what is actual today. The word from the Psalms tells us to count the days so that we will be wise with our decisions.

I love faith and consider myself a man of faith in the foundation of who we are in God, but if we are not careful, we will neglect honesty in developing our plan for financial abundance to match our faith. I created the following plan with God's wisdom to achieve 100% giving in our ministry.

Number one, how many units do we have?

A giving unit can be a single mother, a family, a college student, or a retired senior. Being authentic on these numbers for a correct starting point is priceless for a great start.

Number two, how many are possible now? Not by faith but in reality? According to the stats, the average family in America is three. Please google it for a quick synopsis.

Number three, what is the income of the average family dwelling in a 2-mile radius of your organization? Ours was less than $50,000. That's the income of the household base in a 2-mile radius. You can do this by going to Google, placing your address, and asking it to do it for you.

Number three, Multiply units by 10% of the average family income.

This will speak to your numbers right now.

Below is an example of a 200-person church

Number of units, 200÷3 = 66 possible units

There are 14 giving units now. The American average tells us that 20% of constituents will be givers. The answer is 14 whole tithe and offerings givers who will give according to the average. Mine was $5,000 a year per unit.

The next step, giving 14×5000, is $70,000; the possibility of 66 units times 5000 is 330,000. Please do your math with the equation above and write it out.

With the example given, what is now $70,000. What is possible is $330,000. So, our goal is to increase by $260,000.

What would you do with this continual stream of income? What dream could you see becoming a reality? Plug it in, play it, and figure yours out.

So here is a process for you: The average income in a 2-mile radius —————-. The number of units possible in your organization—————-. 20% of the units = —————-. 100% of the units are —————-. What is possible—————.

ACTION STEP:

Do your numbers, figure it out, and get it correct. What is your possibility? This is what we begin to believe and focus on.

Day 4

Be true to yourself and practice what you preach

- 2 Corinthians 3:2

"You are our letter written in our hearts, known and read by everybody."

People are discerning. People can smell out if the person is saying one thing but doing another. People can tell when you address a subject you know is true, but you are not doing it yourself. I believe the audience can sense it in the back of their minds. Perhaps it is just a hint of disingenuous teaching. Leaders must be true to themselves to speak the truth in authority.

The question then becomes, are you a giver yourself? If one teaches generosity, that person must demand of themselves to be the most generous. If you are a tither, a 10% giver, only then can you genuinely teach the tithe principle.

For those of you who are questioning the tithe or asking what the tithe is, this is to believe that giving 10% of your income to godly ministry, especially to your home church, is a God thing. Remember, we are discussing training your team, congregation, constituents, and anyone who aligns themselves with your nonprofit to become outrageous givers. The end of all things in this subject is that followers will follow but never get ahead of your leadership, so be true to yourself first.

ACTION STEP:

Before you ask others to follow you, ensure you practice good stewardship with your funds, including giving. Are you doing this?

Day 5

Build a process

- Matthew 7:24,25

"Therefore, everyone who hears these words of mine and puts them into practice is like a wise man who built his house on the rock. The rain came down, the streams rose, and the winds blew and beat against the house, yet it did not fail because it had its foundation on the rock."

The process is essential to achieving 100% tithe and creating the income to fund our God-given dreams. We must have a process that becomes our focus year after year. This allows us to put into practice our rock-solid, giving team. Let's outline the five giving steps.

Number one: Those who give nothing cannot believe or lack the means to provide.

Number two: God tippers give funds when it feels good.

Number three: regular givers, giving a specific amount but not the 10%.

Number four: tithing members and followers of Christ who understand 100% the power of the 10% sacrifice.

Five: super tithers who regularly give over 10% and understand the power of complete generosity.

Our process as leaders is to create a system that consistently motivates people to move from no-giving to super-tithers.

Before we leave, let me share my fundamental beliefs about generosity: "A person cannot state that they are a fully devoted follower of Christ without being a dedicated follower, believer, and practitioner of generosity."

It is our job as leaders to work with people in all forms of discipleship.

ACTION STEPS:

Make a chart that works for you that outlines the five steps of giving, which need to be written down. Write it out now.

Day 6

Start with your inner circle

- 2 Sam 23:8a

"These are the names of David's mighty men." Here is a written fact: King David had over 30 mighty men around him, and his predecessor Saul had none." This was David's key to consistent victory in his endeavors.

John Maxwell, the leadership guru of our time, says that "those closest to you determine the level of your success." This is true in all forms of ministry, especially in tithes and offerings; the leader must believe in generosity, and the team surrounding them must also share that unwavering belief. This includes staff, the executive board, and any volunteers on your team.

Shockingly, many who receive paychecks or are responsible for managing resources do not contribute to the organization's vision and goals. Now, this is a gut-check time for you and the leaders. If the leader has been in place for any time, they are responsible for the lack of giving by those closest to them.

The action step involves a three-step process:

One, confession to all teams for your lack of leadership.

Two, outlining the vision and goals for the organization and to the team members mentioned above.

Third, challenge them to join or consider another avenue of ministry.

Leaders, it would be best if you always followed the laws of employment or board selection when issuing a dialogue; perhaps this would take a few years to align all, but it is a must for achieving 100% participation. Action step:

Write down the names of your inner circle, whether paid or volunteer team members.

Day 7

Identify a starting point

- Hebrews 12:1-2

"Therefore, since a great crowd of witnesses surrounds us, let us throw off everything that hinders, and so the sin that is so easily entangled and let us run the race marked out for us. Let us fix our eyes on Jesus, the author and protector of our faith."

Without a starting point, every race will end in a disaster. Most leaders do not fully know where the starting line is. The question that must be answered is exactly what percentage of our constituents are giving now. What is my monthly giving amount for the last 12 months and the previous 24 months? Be honest with yourself about whatever it is. This is your starting point.

Building an organization with 100% participation takes a long-term view. By initiating the systems taught in this book, I aimed to see an increase of 10% year over year. As one progresses in this leadership skill, one should see the first 10% growth happen quickly.

I'm going to be bold here and say that beginning to do things differently with a different and renewed mind results in a quick increase almost immediately.

ACTION STEP:

Do whatever it takes to fully define your starting point so that you can begin helping people become fully devoted followers of Christ.

Day 8

Create an army

- Genesis 14:14

"When Abram heard that his relative had been taken captive, he called out the 318 trained men born in his household and went in pursuit as far as Dan."

Many leaders today hope God will send a homerun financial giver to solve their problems. Early in my ministry career, I heard a great preacher, Tommy Barnett, say, "It's in your house." Our scripture tells us that Abram found it in his house when he needed an army. Most nonprofits have what they need right in their house today. The process of beginning to build a financial fortress to fund your God-given dreams is more than likely right in front of you. The Lord has already set it up for your dream.

I realized that people with the means to give, over and above, don't give but want to invest. Perhaps your army has a mighty man or woman of God waiting for you as a leader to create something worthy of their investment. In the following chapters, we will begin to give you tools for that army in your house.

ACTION STEP:

Please review previous chapters and tighten your thoughts on what you have read. Creating a victorious army of givers starts in your mind and spirit before manifesting in your flesh.

Day 9

Increase in knowledge

- Proverbs 1:7

"The fear of the Lord is the beginning of knowledge, but fools despise wisdom and discipline."

One of the foundational habits that will serve you well in this journey is developing a consistent study process to increase your financial knowledge.

As we increased our giving stream, I found that people wanted to know what I knew, practiced, and learned. As my knowledge in finance grew, more and more people began to give. Givers do not want to provide or invest in a black hole; they want their money to make a difference. They want to believe that you understand what goes on in their daily financial lives.

Do you know what the markets are doing and how they work? How about the knowledge of LLCs, S corporations, or C corporations and the advantages of each one? How do you treat your income and expenses? Do you invest? Are you paying down your debt? Can you direct people to the best resources for their financial situation?

Perhaps you're saying this is too much, and I'm uninterested. I never said developing the resources to fund your God-given dreams would be easy. If it were, you would not be reading this book now, so how do you begin?

ACTION STEP:

Determine to spend 15 minutes a day reading material on investing. Go online, buy a book, read it, then get another and do the same. Ask those in the know what you should study, and make gathering financial knowledge your goal today.

Day 10

Create a personal budget

- Luke 14:28-30

"Suppose one of you wants to build a tower. Will he not first sit down and estimate the cost to see if he has enough money to complete it, for if he lays the foundation and is not able to finish it, everyone who sees it will ridicule him, saying this fellow began to build and was not able to finish".

"Rome was not built in a day," but somebody had to start.

As previously stated, leaders cannot expect their organization to rise above themselves. As we take this journey together, you will learn that many non-givers are that way, not because they do not want to give but because they are in such financial bondage that they cannot see themselves ever getting out of financial prison.

To maintain continuity in our beliefs, if you are a leader and are in bondage, you can never expect to lead successful people into financial abundance and generosity. So, start with yourself today.

This is where most leaders will fail. This is hard because it requires self-examination and perhaps confession to those closest to you, so you must change. Remember the statement we started with that "Rome wasn't built in a day, but somebody had to start?" A true leader begins with themselves.

ACTION STEP:

Find a budgeting tool online and build your budget. You'll be surprised how people will follow you in this endeavor.

Day 11

The father knows best (God)

- Psalms 139:14-16

"I praise you because I am fearfully and wonderfully made. Your words are wonderful; I know that full well. My frame was not hidden from you when I was made in the secret place. When I was woven together in the depths of the earth, your eyes saw my unformed body. All the days ordained for me were written in the book before one of them came to be."

God designed generosity; it is his idea. Do you believe this? Once you do, your actions will begin to tell your belief. God-given ideas to accomplish God-given vision will start to fall into place.

This is the time in our journey when we stop and talk to God differently. This is where we cry out to him that we don't know how to admit our financial failures. Maybe we are discouraged, and we need to let him know. Perhaps our minds are racing with doubt as we journey into the unknown. Maybe you feel shame for how far down the road of lack you have journeyed or praise for how he has brought you this far and how you were looking for guidance for the next step. But whatever it may be or wherever you are, the Father absolutely knows best.

ACTION STEP:

Declare his word over your journey daily using Bible quotes that have already become a foundation in your life, and now add more. Remember, the Bible says, "Build yourself up in the most holy faith." Jude 1:20

Day 12

Stop the bleeding

- 1 Kings 19:21

"So, Elisha left him and went back. He took his yoke on oxen and slaughtered them. He burned the plowing equipment to cook meat and gave it to the people, and they ate. Then he set out to follow Elijah and become his attendant."

Brian was my friend who happened to be an emergency room doctor. We also occasionally played golf together. In one of these games, I asked about medical work in the emergency room. I learned something that has served me well in developing a great giving base that we will explore for the rest of this journey: "When a person comes into an emergency room, and blood is present on that person, the first order of business for the doctor is always to stop the bleeding before a healing process can begin."

For our purpose, let's call it "double-minded." See James 1:8. The process of building an excellent giving machine is to cease being double-minded. Elisha had to burn his plow. We must burn every idea of skipping building income to fund our God-given dreams.

Let's be clear: the journey that we are on is a lifetime journey. My target was to increase giving by 10% year over year, thereby increasing our percentage yearly until our goal was achieved. Ministry has many faces, and giving is just one, but it must be at the forefront of your ministry: prayer, Bible study, discipleship, leadership training, and generosity. All these are the number one priority for you as a leader.

ACTION STEP:

What do you need to burn, and what part of generosity have you let fall by the wayside? Be honest, make up a plan, and let's go forward.

Day 13

Speak life, it's in your words

- Proverbs 18:20

"From the fruit of his mouth, a man's stomach is filled with a harvest from his lips. He is satisfied."

How about this one: "life and death are in the power of the tongue, and those who love it will eat its fruit." Proverbs 18:20. Whatever you think about, study about, or speak about will determine your ministry trajectory; conversely, whatever you don't focus on will fall by the wayside. I will repeat something previously written about in this journal follow-up. A person cannot be entirely devoted to Christ without practicing biblical generosity. Generosity is one of the foundational themes of John 3:16. It says, "For God so loved the world that He gave us His only begotten son."

This might be controversial, but I believe in self-talk, which means talking to myself the way God talks about me, and you must talk about your ministry the way God talks about your ministry.

Below is my daily confession: I am blessed; I have divine favor. I am healthy, wealthy, and full of God's wisdom. I have the mind of Christ. I am generous in our church ministry. Our organization is generous. Our family is giving an abundance. The Lord is training me to grow the ministry and create the funding needed to accomplish more incredible things than I can imagine.

ACTION STEP:

Begin to formulate your thoughts, words, and self-talk; according to Proverbs 18:20, you need to produce fruit first for yourself and then for others.

Day 14

Needs, wants, and desires

- Philippians 4:19 Psalms 37:4

"And my God will meet all your needs according to his generous riches in Christ Jesus." "Delight yourself in the Lord, and he will give you the desires of your heart."

There is no promise in God's word for wants, but we have his commitment to supply our needs and desires, so the question of the day is, why? What desire do you have that needs funding? Your desire will drive you. My passion and my drive were to give more to missions.

For years, the church that I served, Crosswinds AG, couldn't give over 50,000 dollars a year to missions, but I desired to do more, a lot more. This desire drove me to seek the Holy Spirit's help in building a more extensive base over ten years. Our giving to missions grew from 50,000 to over 500,000 dollars from a middle-income to a lower-income community church.

This is the turning point in our journey. From now on, we will add practical steps to build the foundation for the future and practice what we preach.

One last point and question for you: Are your desires correct? Do you want a bigger paycheck, but that is not good enough? So, you can show it off to others, but that is not good enough. If your desires align with God's desires, your supply for the ministry you focus on will follow.

ACTION STEP:

Write down your deepest desires and allow the Holy Spirit to help you. Craft your life-changing moment.

Day 15

Never give up

- Isaiah 54:17

"No weapon formed against you will prevail, and you will refute every tongue that accuses you. This is the heritage of the servants of the Lord, and this is their vindication from me, declares the Lord."

Let's be honest: most of us are great starters, but our finishing is not so good. Perhaps you have read this and are already giving up in your mind. Here is another honest moment. This journey will not be easy because the battle that will rage in your mind will be more complex than the process you are learning.

We have this promise from Isaiah that "no weapon formed against us will prosper:" Even the weapon of war in our minds.

As with anything you begin, please be careful when you share it with others; most will not understand the power of God inside the believers in Christ. God does not show favoritism. Crosswinds AG Church, the church my wife and I served for 31 years, had a higher giving percentage than most protestant churches for our size in America. Here are our numbers from 2023. We had 85% of the church attendance who participated in giving. We gave away 35% of our general fund to missions. We were blessed indeed, but so are you.

ACTION STEP:

Communicate what you believe will be your greatest battle as you build your generosity team.

Day 16

Build a bridge

- Isa. 28:10

"For it is: Do and do, do and do, rule on rule, rule on rule, a little here, a little there."

This chapter begins by building a bridge from your vision, mind, and desires to every person who is and will be walking the journey with you. The bridge will be your method of communication that will become part of you for the rest of your ministry career.

My wife and I have been on a journey for the last 12 months, which has taken us to dozens of churches to see, hear, and observe how they communicate generosity. This also involved us trying to give to every ministry. I said "trying" because sometimes it was downright difficult to provide. Here are two musts in creating generosity, and these two will be your bridge foundation:

Number one, the leader has to be the primary communicator. You cannot give that leadership moment away. I told you this would be hard.

Number two, giving must be accessible; the giver must not be tasked with going on a scavenger hunt for methods to provide to your organization.

Giving checks or cash should be two of six ways to provide for your vision to an organization. I will go over these in detail in the upcoming chapters.

ACTION STEP:

Set yourself up as the primary spokesperson for generosity in your mission.

Day 17

Celebrate victories

- John 2:1,2

"On the third day, a wedding took place at Cana in Galilee. Jesus' mother was there, and Jesus and his disciples had also been invited to the wedding."

As your ministry's primary spokesperson, you celebrate and talk about the victories. People not only want to give, but we believe everybody in Christ wants to be generous. Givers want to know that their sacrifice means something. We need to celebrate together. Almost every week there is something to celebrate. Pace yourself and announce at least one victory per week.

Here is a list of victories that nonprofits will participate in:

A gift to a woman's organization.

A gift to a children's ministry of some sort.

Giving to missionaries in other countries. This list can be very long.

Giving to local charities, such as a regional mission for people experiencing homelessness.

Get involved in your local public school in the neighborhood in which you live.

This list is just a starting point. Understand that the people in your organization have different things that tug on their hearts. And one more thing: just because you are a charity does not mean you should be a taker and not a giver.

ACTION STEP:

Make your list that you will begin to celebrate significant victories publicly regularly.

Day 18

Seeds versus needs

- Genesis 8:22

"As long as the Earth endures seed time and harvest, cold and heat, summer and winter, day and night will never cease."

Your words are your seeds when communicating. Begin to listen to yourself. How are you publicly commenting? Are you speaking in desperate terms? Is it always about paying the light bill? How long have your constituents heard what your organization needs? Investors want a ministry that is making a difference. When your conversation is always about the need, they begin to feel like it will never be filled.

Yesterday's chapter discussed victory, so your words must be seeds of victory. However, you may think I have pressing needs that must be met now. I understand, but if we are going to build successful giving streams, your words must become about what God can and will do both now and in the future.

"God loves a cheerful giver." 2 Corinthians 9:7 says, so give them something to cheer about.

Let's reestablish our truth right now. A person cannot be a fully devoted follower of Christ without being a dedicated giver. Finally, every leader's job is to present a great message, train the staff we have been given, and raise the funds needed to build a great ministry.

ACTION STEP:

Look inside and ask yourself if you genuinely believe the Lord has called you to lead ministry. If so, speak life into the financial arm of that calling in your life.

Day 19

Make it easy

- Matthew 11:30

"For my yoke is easy. My burden is light."

I have previously told you about personally trying to give to every church we visited over the years and finding that most of them made it difficult to give to their ministry. My goal was to provide for every ministry and every nonprofit. Some of them were downright difficult, and we did not give anything.

Setting up your income streams is vital, and I believe that there are six significant ways that every nonprofit should have ready for the giver at all times:

1. Cash giving. Almost everybody has this.
2. Giving by check usually comes from certain aged people, and I am one of them.
3. The internet is set up on your website with a giving pathway.
4. If you are an organization like a church, you must have self-addressed, easy-to-use envelopes that people can take home by adding a stamp and popping them in the

mail. This will allow them to give quickly and easily at home.

5. Texting to give is the second best way for most people to communicate.

6. A one-click Apple Pay on your giving site.

This may seem like a lot of work, but when someone feels like they want to participate in giving, they want to do it immediately, and you also want them to be able to provide it immediately.

ACTION STEP:

Check your systems now. If you are a missionary, a pastor, or a nonprofit, create a link to any of the six outlined ways and start working on it today.

Day 20

Providing training weekly, monthly, or yearly is a priority

- 1Cor. 9: 24-25

"Do you not know that all the runners run in a race, but only one gets the prize? Run in such a way as to get the prize. Everyone who competes in games goes into strict training. They do it to get a crown that will not last, but we do it to get one that will last forever."

Training yourself, your team, and your constituents is an ongoing process that must be presented weekly, monthly, and yearly.

The weekly training is like an archer; let's call it arrow messages. We do not spend in-depth time on it but ensure it is spoken of in many ways.

The monthly training is for staff and team members to ensure they always feel your heart and understand your organization's vision of abundance. This should take 30 minutes to an hour every month.

Yearly is when you take three weeks to a month to deliver and develop a strategy for debt reduction and generosity development of every person in your organization. If you're in a church setting, this will mean preaching a series every year that sets up a target that your weekly arrow can shoot at. As a practice, I believe that February is the best month to do this ministry.

People are thinking about finances because of all the stuff hanging over them in the new year, and they're looking for biblical clarity on debt reduction, saving, and investing.

ACTION STEP:

Go to your personal and professional calendar, schedule your yearly preaching or talking point, and begin to work backward, scheduling monthly and weekly arrow points.

Day 21

You are what you read

- Colossians 3:2,3

"Set your mind on things above, not on earthly things, for you died, and your life is now hidden with Christ in God."

Readers are leaders. I believe John Maxwell said this. It is a vital truth that when you are on a journey of change, it begins in the mind and spirit and then manifests in the body. If you want to become excellent at developing the financial foundation that you need to find your God-given dreams and visions, then a steady diet of financial reading is a must.

Your giving team will consist of all types of people, from the widow with a fixed income to the person with a multi-million dollar corporation. You need to be able to talk to everyone with the same kind of financial intelligence. You do not need to be the expert, but you should bring understanding to the table in whatever room you find yourself in.

Read about debt reduction, personal budgeting, business building, understanding the corporate structure, what millionaires think and how they conduct themselves, and why and when corporate businesses invest in nonprofits or church giving. This is not an exhaustive list, but it should give you a general understanding.

What separates this from Chapter 9 is that this moment is very personal. We read not to look outward but to gaze at our inward selves and ensure that we grow personally.

Regarding people's financial lives, I have found that big givers are more interested in my leadership understanding, including my financial knowledge, what I'm doing about it, and how I live, more than my standing in my organization, so read, read.

ACTION STEP:

Start reading 15 minutes of financial literature daily.

Day 22

Ask for help

- Matthew 7:7

"Ask, and it will be given to you; seek, and you will find; knock, and the door will be open to you."

We don't know it all! To believe that we do is the foundation of ignorance. We don't go to an MD to get our teeth worked on or hire an electrician to fix our plumbing similarly; not all are financial experts. Just because you are a pastor or nonprofit leader does not mean you know how to raise money, or as I have found out, none of my ministry training in my college degree ever taught me how to create a great giving organization. One of the greatest freedoms I have ever experienced was the day I confessed these words: "I don't know."

We are talking about a 100% tithe base here. The reading of this manual is the first step. Perhaps you need to bring somebody alongside who has done it and can help you identify where you are weak, opening your eyes to the areas you have messed up or are missing and building your base of givers. The day I reached out and got help for my lack of understanding of what it means to be a good husband, father, and friend was a day of victory. How about you? This is a selfless promotion here, but if you need help identifying where you are financially weak and how to go forward, please don't hesitate to contact me. My contact information is at the end of this book.

ACTION STEP:

If you need help, ask for it, and don't allow your pride to stop your momentum.

Day 23

Get a tow truck when you get stuck

- 2 Peter 1:3a

"Therefore, prepare your mind for action, be self-controlled, and set your hope fully on the grace to be given to you when Jesus Christ is revealed."

As I have stated, I developed my income stream because I love foreign and stateside missions. However, we were stuck for ten straight years at giving $50,000 to missions per year, and indeed, I needed a spiritual and mental tow truck to get me off the $50,000 mark.

My tow truck, and I think most of us, was that I had to become so aggravated, sick, and tired, or whatever you want to call it, that I began asking God to reveal why we were stuck. This is where and when I encountered Jack Hayford for the epiphany moment. I was sick and tired, and revelation brought about change.

How have you grown personally, professionally, or corporately in the last five or ten years? Are you ready for a breakthrough? This is your moment, so do not let it pass you by. The fact that you have made it this far means you are ready.

This is our spiritual time out today. Let the coach, the holy spirit, speak. I have found that our Lord wants to communicate but will not hesitate or waste his voice on those who will not listen.

ACTION STEP:

Get alone and pray verbally. Ask the Lord to give you a hundred percent givers of tithe and offerings, or if you are a nonprofit or outside the local church, ask him to increase your knowledge of attracting donors. Look for your tow truck.

Day 24

"Rome was not built in a day"

- Ecclesiastes 3:11a

"He has made everything beautiful in his time."

It takes time to do this right and achieve your desired results. I know that you're probably desperate or despise the last statement. We all have pressing desires and needs, but I am sure we want lasting desires more than our momentary needs.

My wife and I were blessed to visit Rome a few years ago. While we were there, we visited the Palace grounds of the Caesars. We learned that every new Caesar would build and connect his quarters to the existing palace homes. This area is composed of acres; it wasn't built in a day, but generation upon generation added to the foundation set by their predecessors.

Great giving streams are like this: Set your mind on an achievable goal of a 10% increase year over year. Let the Lord work with you to perfect your vision and build your process. So far, through these pages, we have given you building blocks. Be patient as you work on yourself and your team; your process will increase. Your dream has a solution, and the Lord has set it before you. I experience that these tools only produce results when you are persistent and patient.

ACTION STEP:

Make a goal to increase your income by 10% in the next 12 months. To do that, work on your base now and come up with the actual numbers to start with.

Day 25

The power of FPU

- 2Tim 2:15

"Do your best to present yourself to God as one approved workman who does not need to be ashamed and who correctly handles the word of truth."

As I said earlier, I believe that most people want to be generous, but they can't because they have taken a financial path that has put them into slavery and debt. Isn't this the American way? Once a person or family finds themselves in this predicament, they probably feel awful because they cannot give generously in obedience to the Lord's process of giving. This is where you, as a leader, can provide them with hope.

Out of all the chapters we have explained, this one is vital in building a solid generosity team. It is called FPU, Financial Peace University, and Dave Ramsey wrote it. He has created the best debt reduction method that all ministers can use. Almost everyone reading this has probably heard of Dave Ramsey and FPU.

I haven't received anything from this company for promotion, but we have offered FPU in our church for 15 years. Even during the COVID shutdown, we purchased 1500 online classes and provided free access to our constituents who were in lockdown. It was and is a ray of hope for those in the debt cycle.

God's message is always one of hope, and we leaders must be purveyors of hope when we teach generosity. We must always give hope to those caught in the debt trap.

ACTION STEP:

Research FPU on the Internet and set up your avenue of hope today. Also, make sure that you and your team take these classes so you can practice what you preach and talk about it intelligently. This is vital.

Day 26

Millionaire maker

- 1Timothy 4:8

"Physical training is of some value, but godliness has value for all things, holding promise for both the present and the life to come."

Right here, I'm going to say something that will probably be controversial, but what I believe is 100% true: If a person practices biblical stewardship in their personal life, avoiding debt and investing correctly, they cannot help but become wealthy. There are just too many scriptures to back up this statement.

The next step came after we at Crosswinds saw people getting out of debt, paying off their mortgages, and becoming debt-free. We needed the next step. How will we develop mighty men and women of God into becoming what I call super tithers? This brought about a class that we entitled the millionaire maker class; this class was devoted to next-level wealth building and the next level the people of God need to take. We must offer this training in our organizations, taking financial training back from the world. The world has some fantastic training available to all, but why not provide this in our ministries as we build our giving base?

I can hear you saying right now that I can never do this. Yes, you can. You become what you want others to become and lead the way. As your giving team grows, you will need to be the leader and not just the wisher, wishing that God would give you great givers. People will follow two steps behind the leader, never in front of the leader. I would be happy to share class outlines with you, but let me say that an opening class would always start with this statement. "We want you to become wealthy to become outrageous givers."

ACTION STEP:

Place your financial plan on a trajectory toward millionaire status. Yes, you can do this.

Day 27

Bring it home

- Eph 5:19-20

"Speak to one another with psalms and hymns and spiritual songs, singing, and make music in your heart to the Lord, always giving thanks to God, the Father, for everything in the name of our Lord Jesus Christ."

Every spiritual leader has three primary purposes: 1. to continue to become a great communicator. 2. to train the team that God has placed in your hands, especially if they are volunteers, and never despise anyone willing to follow you. 3. raise the funds needed to bring your God-given dreams into reality. Number three is what we are focusing on here.

Beat these three purposes into your mind through the Holy Spirit's leading and bring them home. This is what we mean by this title: make your purpose strong, allowing your team to get on the purpose train with you. Your communication skills never arrive, but you'll always strive to hone them in yourself and improve at communicating and training your team. Finally, your fundraising skills will always need to improve, but you will do everything possible to become the leader with more than enough to accomplish your dream.

When we say "bring it home," we mean don't settle for good enough. Put a laser beam on your leadership process. Bring it home; bring it home to yourself.

ACTION STEP:

Out of the three steps in this chapter, examine yourself and design your plan for momentum. We could all use more work, so let's do it. Let's become the person we know God has called us to be.

Day 28

Start over again and again

- Philippians 3:12

"Not that I have already obtained all this or I've already been made perfect, but I press in to take hold of that which Christ Jesus took hold of me. "

Upon retirement from Pastoral ministry, our missions increased 10 X, and our giving base was 85% of regular attendees. I will be forever grateful for this. The key was starting the journey in January, reviewing our process, and making goals that everybody was on board with. Our personal and professional financial goals also included this. This is called reset.

Never assume that you and every other team member are still tracking with the vision of 100% constituents on the giving train. This was what I said, and it became my motivation. The first week in January, we began with the complete financial checkup in staff meetings to get on the debt reduction path, if needed, ensuring everyone was aligned with our method. We also celebrated victories throughout the year as team members achieved their goals. Essentially, we started again and again and again.

On the first week of February, we began our yearly teaching on our financial ministry to our constituents, outlining steps to financial victory for all of us. This was our avenue to creating and building income to pursue God-given dreams. Starting FPU at this time was perfect. The job is never done if you keep your dreams and visions at the forefront of your mind. The development of resources will be a joy and exciting.

ACTION STEP:

Begin again and put together your plan for your vision and dreams.

Day 29

Reevaluate your why

- 1John 2:17

"The world and its desires pass away, but the man who does the will of God lives forever."

As we progress and flourish, our why will morph and change. Perhaps you have completed some goals. Maybe you finished one race and are starting another. As your giving base grows, new opportunities you never believed possible will open up.

One must always have a why, but your why doesn't have to stay the same. Like yesterday's chapter on starting over again, this must happen, and revealing your why must be a yearly process. Maybe it will stay the same for five, six, or seven years or change after year one.

Perhaps your original why was the catalyst needed by the Holy Spirit to get you to change and move into new blessings. Always work on his purpose; his revelation is progressive as you grow. As you grow, the revelation grows, the team grows, and the needs grow. You are becoming what you thought would never happen.

As our mission-giving grew, so did the doors of opportunity open. The why guided us to say yes to some and no to others.

ACTION STEP:

Write down a vision card that you would do with an organization with a double portion of income.

Day 30

Bring as many people with you as possible

- Matthew 4:19

"Come follow me, Jesus said, and I will make you fishers of men."

When you start this journey, keep it to yourself, but share it with others as the Lord blesses your mission.

The writing of this 30-day devotional exists for this very reason: We do not lord it over others to say how great we are. We celebrate the God of victories in a way that lifts others to join us on this journey.

Jack Hayford's one-hour lecture changed my life forever. I hope that you are encouraged to believe that it is possible.

The Holy Spirit did not place visions and dreams in our heart that would die, but that they will flourish and be able to do "immeasurably more than we can ask, think, and imagine according to his will that has worked with us." Ephesians 3:20 says.

At the beginning of your journey, I encouraged you to build an income to fund your dreams, prepare yourself as your income grows, and begin to take as many as possible with you. I believe that this is the Holy Spirit's way. We don't live on an island but are part of a worldwide team with whom the Lord deals daily. All we need to do is do our part.

ACTION STEP:

Quit saying you can't because you "can do everything through Christ who strengthens you." Philippians 4:13, and so we come to an end. I hope you are encouraged and believe God can do great things through you.

Conclusion

At the time of this writing, I am a retired minister from full-time pastoral ministry after 40 years of service. It has been a fantastic wild ride that the Lord has allowed my wife Janet and I to participate in. We have one regret: we only have one life to live for God's glory.

If I could go back in time, I would change only a few things: That we could have the one hundred percent giving process right from the start of our ministry. Still, the Lord knew the right time for us; I believe it is your time now. Take it to heart, and if we can help you, please don't hesitate to ask, for we "have not because we ask not." James 4:3. "You are blessed. You have divine favor. You're not alone. You're a child of God. You are more than a conqueror. You walk in the promises of God's holy word, for God has a miracle for you." Pete Vossler

I told you a few times in this book that I would give you a way to contact us for consulting, speaking, coaching, or team development. You can email me at pjanet@mac.com.

Made in the USA
Las Vegas, NV
08 February 2025

17705540R00039